——— Hawker's ———
MORWENSTOW

MICHAEL WILLIAMS

BOSSINEY BOOKS

First published in 1988 by
Bossiney Books
St Teath, Bodmin, Cornwall.

Typeset and Printed by
Clowes Book Printers
St Columb, Cornwall.

Front cover by Ray Bishop:
Morwenstow Church
Back cover by Ray Bishop:
Morwenstow Vicarage

PLATE ACKNOWLEDGMENTS
Ray Bishop: pages 1, 5, 7, 11, 15, 19, 20, 21, 23, 26, 28, 30-35, 38, 39, 41, 47-53, 55, 57, 58-62

Felicity Young: pages 22, 25 lower, 37, 40, 56, 57

Local Studies Library, Redruth: pages 8, 13, 17, 24, 25 upper, 29, 63

Paul Honeywill: page 54

The Cornish Guardian: page 46

Acknowledgements

In the early summer of 1988, a conversation at Rectory Farm revealed the urgent need for a new Bossiney title on *Hawker's Morwenstow* – something very visual, showing places connected with the great man in his 41 years here. This publication is the result. I am especially indebted to Joanne Hillman at the Local Studies Library at Redruth for help in finding Hawker material and Terry Knight for permission to use some old photographs. Joan Rendell's *Hawker Country*, published by Bossiney in 1980, and out of print for some years, remains essential reading for anyone interested in this corner of Cornwall.

Bibliography

Hawker of Morwenstow by the Reverend H. Hugh Breton MA 1927

Hawker Country by Joan Rendell 1980

Hawker of Morwenstow by Piers Brendon 1975

About the Author and the Book

A Cornishman, Michael Williams started full-time publishing in 1975. With his wife Sonia, he runs Bossiney Books from a cottage and converted barn in North Cornwall – they are literally cottage publishers, specialising in Westcountry subjects by Westcountry authors. For ten years they ran the Bossiney House Hotel, just outside Tintagel – hence the name Bossiney Books.

In addition to publishing and writing, Michael Williams is a keen cricket enthusiast and collector of cricket books. He is President of the Cornish Crusaders Cricket Club and a member of the Cornwall and Gloucestershire County Clubs. He is also a member of the RSPCA, and has actively worked for reform in laws relating to animal welfare. In 1984, he was elected to the Ghost Club, and remains convinced Cornwall is the most haunted area in the whole of Great Britain.

His most recent publications are *Supernatural Adventure, Widecombe* and *St Ives.* As a publisher, he recently launched his first Dorset titles and a third Dorset book is to appear early in 1989. Bossiney now covers five areas: Cornwall, Devon, Dorset, Somerset and Avon.

In *Hawker's Morwenstow,* Michael Williams tours a corner of North Cornwall immortalized by Robert Stephen Hawker who was vicar here for 41 years. All the presentday photographs by Ray Bishop and the drawings by Felicity Young have been especially commissioned. These, plus some rare old photographs, combine to give a grand visual tour. 'Hawker's Morwenstow', says the author, 'has a haunted, haunting atmosphere . . . you sense he has never left the place.' Coombe, Welcombe, The Bush Inn, Duckpool, Rectory Farm, Hawker's Hut and his celebrated Vicarage are only some of the places featured on a journey which takes us back in time and mood.

Hawker's Morwenstow

Hawker's Morwenstow has a haunted, haunting atmosphere.

This is contrasting country: deep, wooded coombe and towering jagged cliffs; ablaze with flowers in season, then robbed of colour; invaded by visitors but often almost deserted in winter. It's a first or last corner of Cornwall before Welcombe and England begins.

'Here,' said Sir John Betjeman, 'one is reaching not only the end of Cornwall, but it seems the end of the world.'

This north eastern tip of Cornwall is truly a remote triangle of landscape, separated from Devon and England by the upper reaches of the Tamar Valley. They say the Saxons never overwhelmed the Celtic Cornish – and you get this feeling of a separate identity here – maybe intensified by the fact that the border is so near.

Robert Stephen Hawker was at Morwenstow for more than forty years and you sense he has never left the place. Some people are convinced Hawker still haunts his old parish. One such character was Constance Drummond of Stratton who recalled: 'One evening a friend and I were walking back from Morwenstow with my retriever dog. We *both* heard footsteps behind us. There was a corner, and we both paused. I said: "Oh, let's wait for whoever it is to pass." We stopped and noticed that my dog had flattened himself into the hedge. The footsteps came on round the corner, passed us, and went on. No-one to be seen. At a cottage higher up, I asked a woman if the lane was haunted. "Oh, yes," she said brightly, "Parson Hawker often comes up after being at the church ..."'

There is no real Morwenstow village.

The parish, sprawling across something like 7,000 acres, is essentially a matter of a few hamlets: Woodford and Woolley, Crosstown and Shop, Gooseham and Eastcott and finally West Youlstone – though not quite finally for there are the ancient manor

4

houses of Tonacombe, Marsland and Stanbury and the isolated farms, the Bush Inn too. All are linked by delightful narrow twisting lanes. 'The lonely Farthest North of England's Farthest South,' Arthur Mee called it.

Made a deacon in 1829 and ordained in 1831, Robert Stephen Hawker came to Morwenstow in 1834. He came, in the words of a contributor to *John Bull,* to 'a manse in ruins, and partly used as a barn; a parish peopled by wreckers and dissenting Bryanites; and a venerable church, deserted and ill-cared for amidst a heap of weeds and nettles.'

Here he remained for the next 41 years, turning Morwenstow into 'his' kingdom. The fact is Hawker was more than a parson. He was an all-rounder: he made things happen. He built the vicarage, restored the church.

A poet and author, he gained immortality in the Westcountry with *The Song of the Western Men:*

> *And shall Trelawny die?*
> *Then twenty thousand Cornishmen*
> *Will know the reason why!*

An innovator too, in 1843 Hawker called upon his flock: 'Let us gather together in the chancel of our church on the first Sunday of next month, and there receive, in the bread of the new corn, that blessed sacrament which was ordained to strengthen and refresh our souls.' So on the first Sunday of October that year Hawker launched the modern Harvest Festival.

Not for nothing did Robert Stephen Hawker write:

> *From Hartland Point to Padstow Light*
> *Is a watery grave by day and by night.*

The simple truth is this *is* a wicked coastline. Between 1824 and 1874, the year in which the lighthouse on Hartland Point was built, there were more than eighty wrecks in the area. In 1832 an old resident of

RIGHT Morwenstow Cliffs. This stretch of coastline has been the graveyard of many ships and the scene of heroic deeds in rescue.

Poughhill near Bude wrote an account of some 37 wrecks between Morwenstow and St Gennys in less than a hundred years.

Hawker will always be remembered for his Christian burial of men who died in the wrecks. Describing the churchyard in 1870 he wrote: 'Along and beneath the southern trees, side by side, are the graves of between thirty and forty seamen, hurled by the sea in shipwrecks and gathered up and buried there by the present vicar and his people.'

In one letter, he showed just what a gruesome business it all was: 'And the search for the bodies still goes on. Limbs are cast ashore every now and then, arms and legs, and at Hartland, adjoining Welcombe, lumps of flesh have floated above high water and been buried in the ground. Five out of seven corpses had no heads, cut off by the jagged rocks! It is indeed a fearful country to inhabit.'

Once Hawker wrote of being roused at first light of day by a boy: 'In a moment I was up, and in my cassock and slippers rushed out. There stood my lad, weeping bitterly, and holding out to me in his trembling hands a tortoise, alive. I found afterwards that he had grasped it on the beach, and brought it in his hand as a strange and marvellous arrival from the waves, but in utter ignorance of what it might be.

'I ran across my glebe, a quarter of a mile, to the cliffs, and down a frightful descent of 300 feet to the beach. It was, indeed, a scene to be looked on only once in a human life. On a ridge of rock, just left bare by the falling tide, stood a man, my own servant: he had come out to see my flock of ewes, and had found the awful wreck. There he stood, with two dead sailors at his feet, whom he had just drawn out of the water, stiff and stark.'

Nothing symbolizes Hawker's ministry at Morwenstow more poignantly than the strange white monument, on the left above the narrow path which slopes down the churchyard to the main door. It is the figurehead of the *Caledonia*, a two-hundred-ton sailing ship from Arbroath which ran aground nearby in a terrible gale in 1842. There was only one survivor. All the other men aboard died and Hawker, to his considerable credit, located every body and buried them here.

Joan Rendell, the Cornish Bard and author of *Hawker Country,* published by Bossiney in 1980 and now out of print for several years, recalled: 'He (Hawker) also saved the ship's figurehead, a wooden figure of a native Caledonian in the dress of Scotland at that period and complete with shield and sword. The figurehead Mr Hawker placed over the grave of the ship's captain and there it stands to this day, still well preserved and carefully looked after by those who worship at Morwenstow today. Various superstitions have grown up around it and although they are only superstitions there are still those in the neighbourhood who believe them, although they will probably not be anxious to admit to it!

'In October 1968 the *Caledonia* figurehead disappeared from the churchyard and there was great consternation. Police found it three weeks later, abandoned in a field at Abbotsham Cross, near Bideford. The police replaced it in the churchyard and there was great relief all round. The figurehead had been slightly damaged: the shield and one foot had been broken off and the already broken tip of the sword had been removed, but a fund was soon started to provide enough cash for the figurehead to be restored to its original condition. Because hundreds of Scottish visitors go to Morwenstow each year to see the figurehead of the Caledonian warrior, the police enquiries into the disappearance were pursued as far as Arbroath itself, but the culprits were never brought to book. There was a suggestion that the thieves intended to take the figurehead out of the country, where it would fetch a high price on the American market, and Mr Jim Gregory, licensee of the nearby Bush Inn, was quoted at the time as saying that he believed no local inhabitant would have removed the figurehead because, he said, "they wouldn't be seen within a hundred yards of it at night, they regard it both with awe and dread".

'So what is this strange power that the *Caledonia* figurehead has? Having already said that various superstitions have grown up around the object, it can now be revealed that what many local people hesitate to put into words, even when pressed, is that they believe that if one walks in an anti-clockwise direction around the figurehead

RIGHT The 'Caledonia' figurehead above the path in Morwenstow Churchyard: a monument to Hawker's remarkable ministry.

thirteen times the spirits of the shipwrecked sailors will rise up and the figure will strike out with its sword. No, this writer has never tested it – *she* is Cornish too! What is probably a rational explanation is that the Reverend Hawker himself invented and spread the story in order to discourage morbid curiosity and the presence of sightseers to what was to him a very sacred spot.'

Today, Hawker would be in the vanguard of the animal welfare movement. He loved all animals. The local birds became so tame that they fluttered around him to be fed and, in one of his letters, he referred to a pair of mice playing on his desk while he was writing! He lived, of course, in days before the motor car and travelled by horse, either riding or driving. He had two horses called Brychan and Gladys, named after the mother and father of St Morwenna. Until his last years he invariably rode to Welcombe which he looked after as well as Morwenstow for a quarter of a century – right up until just before his death in fact. In his last declining years he drove a pair of ponies. He had, for some years, a faithful dog Berg, and whenever he went to the church Berg went with him carrying the church key in his mouth which he delivered into the parson's hand at the church door. Usually several cats accompanied him into the chancel. At one time, too, he kept a pig called Gyp who travelled miles with him. As jackdaws nested in the strangely beautiful chimneys of Morwenstow vicarage, fires were forbidden in certain rooms for fear of dislodging the birds. Hawker was also concerned when a neighbour shot one or two rooks which had been reared in the churchyard. On the following Sunday, the neighbour, seated in the front pew, received the dressing down of his life. Hawker's text, that Sunday, was 'Are not two sparrows sold for a farthing? And one of them shall not fall to the ground without your Father.' No more rooks were shot.

But of all the animals in his life his special favourite was Carrow his pony. According to local legend he lavished more care on Carrow than his wife! That is almost certainly an injustice, but he loved the animal dearly. Carrow resided in a stable at the vicarage and, on duty, was either ridden by his master or harnessed to a little vehicle. They must have travelled hundreds of miles together on their journeys around this border territory.

RIGHT Not Hawker's Morwenstow but his birthplace: 6 Norley Street, Plymouth, Devon.

12

On one dramatic occasion they were travelling from Welcombe back to Morwenstow and Hawker recalled: 'As I entered the Gulph between the Vallies today, a Storm leaped from the Sea, and rushed at me roaring – I recognised a Demon and put Carrow into a gallop and so escaped.'

Hawker, throughout his life, was very preoccupied with the mystical and the Supernatural. Like many young men, he had hoaxed on the subject; pretending to be a mermaid, he hoodwinked people at Bude. For several nights the mermaid appeared, flashing her mirror and singing strange songs, and the number of inquisitive people multiplied. Hawker, however, tired of sitting in the cold night air, clad only in seaweed – the mermaid never appeared again.

Later in his ministry, though, he claimed genuine Supernatural experience to the extent of *seeing* Saint Morwenna and, over the years, he became convinced in the power of the Evil Eye, once attributing the loss of nine suckling-pigs to a witch's curse. 'The sow which, like Medea, had taken a hatred to her own offspring, spurning them away from her milk . . . the evil eye of old Cherry (the witch) had turned the mother's heart to stone, and she let them die one by one . . .'

Healing and charming, dowsing and ley lines, all these are fashionable subjects in North Cornwall today. We can guess that mysticism and allied Occult subjects dominated in Hawker's day too. Not surprising then that the great man should have written a book entitled *Ghosts*. Morwenstow surely is such a place to trigger ideas along those eerie lines. In his reign it must have been an even more remote place – had a more haunted air.

Hawker himself defies the easy pigeon hole. He was quite simply a cleric of many parts and, at a deeper level, he was an enigma too. Unorthodox and unconventional, learned and impulsive, generous and indiscreet – he was all these and a great deal more. Like his grandfather, Dr Hawker of Charles Church, Plymouth, he was ready to give away almost everything he had. On wild winter nights he would have curious intuitions about those who might need some extra food or bed covering. Prompted by such inner feelings, he would gather together blankets, food and even wine and, accompanied by a servant, would set out and subsequently knock at the door of the cottage in question.

Physically, he was tall and well-built, his voice so rich and

ABOVE The memorial cross in the churchyard to Charlotte Hawker, his wife for nearly forty years. Her influence was considerable.

15

powerful that he could carry on a conversation with a neighbour at a farm on the other side of the valley.

Chunks of Hawker's life read like fiction rather than fact. His two marriages could scarcely have been more contrasting. He was an undergraduate at Oxford University when he married his first wife, Charlotte, a daughter of Colonel Wrey I'ans of Whitstone who was his godmother – then aged 41! In his University days, married, it was arranged his wife's two sisters should come to live with them and he became known as 'the man with three wives'!

The influence of Charlotte was considerable. A woman of poetic, refined mind, she helped him through times of depression giving him sound guidance when impetuosity robbed him of balanced judgement. She was his wife for nearly forty years and her passing wounded him deeply.

However he found happiness in a second marriage. It says much for his attractive personality that he was able to woo and wed an intelligent and high spirited girl forty years his junior. Pauline Kuczynski, the daughter of an English lady married to an exiled Pole, was employed as a governess to a Yorkshire vicar's children. They came to Morwenstow when the Reverend W. Valentine needed to convalesce in the sea air of North Cornwall.

Hawker fell deeply in love with the younger woman who bore him three daughters. The feelings were mutual, but it is said he was saddened by the fact that she failed to produce a son.

In the last years, Hawker's health declined seriously; the prospects of his family oppressed him, anxieties gnawed. In June, 1875, he stayed with his brother at Boscastle, who, in a letter, described him as 'very ill, and certainly broken in his mind'. By the end of August, Robert Stephen Hawker was in his coffin in Plymouth Cemetery – a Roman Catholic. His end is cloaked in confusion and controversy.

RIGHT Pauline, the second Mrs Hawker. He adored her and wrote of her: '. . . a young woman with a Face and Form to win an Emperor.' However she remains a central tantalising figure in the controversy surrounding his death-bed conversion to the Roman Catholic Church.

The second Mrs Hawker – Pauline – had taken him to Plymouth for medical advice. There he had suffered a paralytic stroke, and on the Saturday before his death, Mrs Hawker sent for the Roman Catholic, Canon Mansfield. She later insisted that such an invitation was at the request of her husband. Sabine Baring-Gould, though, in his biography *The Vicar of Morwenstow* clearly stated: 'Through the kindness of Mr Hawker's relatives I have been furnished with every letter that passed on the subject of his death, and reception into Roman communion. In not one of them is it asserted that he asked to have Canon Mansfield sent for: the last expression of a wish was that he might go back to Morwenstow.'

Baring-Gould's biography, it is fair to say, does contain some inaccuracies. But that wish to 'go back to Morwenstow' has an authentic ring. Hawker, after all, had given 41 years of his life to the parish. Nevertheless Pauline Hawker should have known her husband's innermost thoughts. Or did she? Her belief was that he had been 'at heart a Roman Catholic' for some years.

Was Hawker capable of making a decision to join the Roman Catholic Church at this sick, late stage in his life? Or did he hang on at Morwenstow because he loved the place so? Or did he stay for purely material reasons? Or did he profess Roman Catholicism privately and yet publicly perform as an Anglican parson?

These are only some of the questions that shape themselves in what was a religious row and remains a riddle surrounding Hawker's earthly end. We shall probably never now get to the bottom of it. This much is certain: in the hearts of many Cornish people, Hawker will – for ever – be the Vicar of Morwenstow.

In a scenic sense, Morwenstow Church stands in a beautiful location. Shortly before Hawker's death, a certain parson expressed the view it was a pity the church had not been built in a more central part of the parish whereby it could attract larger congregations. Hawker, however, would have none of it: 'In the days they built this church,' he thundered, 'they built not for congregations, but DEI GLORIA.'

His beloved church. Where better to begin our tour of Hawker's Morwenstow?

RIGHT A view of the church from the ground in front of the vicarage.

Morwenstow Church

RIGHT The Church, seen from the field on the seaward side. Hawker, like the Normans long before him, felt the power of the place – and left his mark upon it. Sir John Betjeman, visiting here, felt Hawker's 'strong Celtic, catholic and compassionate personality pervades this remote parish and particularly its church and glebe.'

There is a delightful story about the occasion when a rather pompous Archdeacon of Bodmin on a visit enquired: 'And what are your views, Mr Hawker?' The guest was promptly taken to the sitting room window and his host, with a familiar waft of the hand, declared: 'These are my views. My opinions I keep to myself!'

ABOVE This, for many people, is their first impression of Hawker's Morwenstow: the entrance to the churchyard.

LEFT Felicity Young's drawing of the magnificent main door, surely one of the most noble entrances in all Cornwall. The church is dedicated to St Morwenna. Hawker perpetuated the legend – some say he invented it! – that the Saint was the daughter of Breachan, a Celtic King who lived in the ninth century. Moreover the parson claimed that he had seen Saint Morwenna. As for the name Morwenstow, according to Piers Brendon, Hawker's admirable biographer, it is a marriage of 'Celtic "Morwen" (possibly meaning "white or fair as the sea" or perhaps derived from St Morwenna) and the Saxon "stow" (church).'

BELOW Here is Charlotte Hawker's grave, outside the chancel. 'There is sprung up a light for the righteous, and joyful gladness for such as are true-hearted.' The text refers to her blindness.

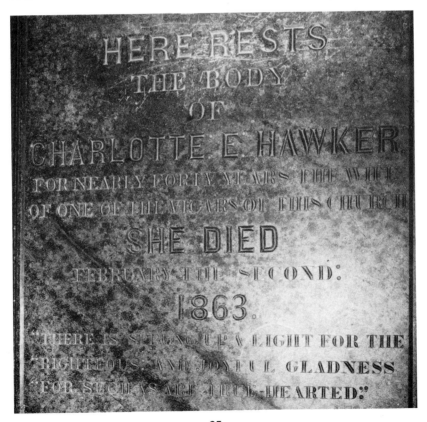

ABOVE AND ABOVE RIGHT Two aspects of the interior of
Morwenstow Church.

Robert Stephen Hawker loved his church dearly and he was capable
of giving significance to the smallest detail, of almost turning the
prosaic into poetry. He maintained the zigzags, situated near the font,
were 'the ripple of the lake of Gennesaret, the spirits breathing upon
the waters of baptism'.

Joan Rendell in her *Hawker Country* has made another interesting
point about the church: '. . . if one stands square on the step leading
into the belfry tower and then looks towards the east end of the
church there is a distinct impression that the church is one sided.'
Again Hawker had a theory: 'As Christ upon the Cross, His head
inclined, so His sanctuary is built with an inclination to one side.'

Hawker's spirit still lives on inside these walls. Fact is there is
plenty to catch the eye, quicken the imagination too. Even a

RIGHT Details of stonework in the Church.

hardbitten *Sunday Times* reporter once mistook the sound of an ancient vacuum cleaner for that of a transistor set! Hawker, of course, might have forgiven that in the light and sound of *some* modern music.

The Primitive Methodist Quarterly Review, published back in 1905, gives us some clues about Hawker's interpretations:

> 'Suggestive of the inherent strength of Hawker's genius is the circumstance that the seclusion of his life for over forty years at a lonely Cornish village did not extinguish his poetical powers, although it may have had the effect of strengthening his eccentricities. But from his enthusiastic love of the romantic and marvellous, from his passion for the traditions and events connected with the wild and beautiful features of the scenery of the district, sprang up that reverent delight which found expression in his ballads as well as in prose sketches of rare quaintness and charm...'

Quaint language no doubt – but almost certainly containing essential truths about this paradox of a parson.

LEFT Hawker cut an impressive figure at church services. Robed in beautiful vestments, he administered rites with great dignity, but there was invariably the human element in his ministry. For example, during the Sacrament of Holy Baptism he had the habit of pinching the child to make it squeal 'to let the Devil out...' At a wedding too he had a little ritual of tossing the ring into the air and catching it 'for luck for the happy couple'.

He could, though, be caustic. A dissenter came to him one day: someone who had just lost a relative. 'Bury a dissenter,' replied the Parson, 'I shall be delighted. I should like to bury the lot!'

Often he had services on weekdays, and when the moment came for the sexton to cease ringing, Hawker would shout down the church: 'Now, John, three for the Trinity and one for The Blessed Virgin!' Then the service would commence.

27

Hawker's Vicarage

Hawker's greatest material achievement in the parish was the building of the Vicarage in 1837. He built it with his own money – a costly operation – and, as a result, he was a poor man for the rest of his life.

The Reverend Hugh Breton, MA, Vicar of Morwenstow, in his booklet *Hawker of Morwenstow* published in 1927, price one shilling, postage two pence, had this to say:

'When he came to Morwenstow, the parish had not known a resident vicar for more than a century. The old Vicarage, which stood above the Church, was used partly as a barn, and was in a state of almost utter ruin – so bad that repair and restoration were impossible.

'So he decided to build the new Vicarage on another site, and he chose the present one, because he said he always noticed that it was where the sheep and lambs lay down, suggesting that it must be a place of shelter. In many ways the site has proved a wise choice, for

29

the water supply comes into the house by natural fall from St John the Baptist's Well in the garden, and the drainage leaves the house by natural fall into the valley below.

'The boards he used for flooring are thick pitch-pine of unusual width, the likes of which are not seen in these days; the doors are finely made and studded with great nails. He built the house regardless of expense, but he found out afterwards what was the cost of doing work so well. Over the front door he placed the inscription:

> A house, a glebe, a pound a day;
> A pleasant place to watch and pray;
> Be true to Church, be kind to poor,
> O minister! for evermore.

'Five of the chimneys are models of Towers of Parish Churches where he had lived before, and the kitchen chimney represents his Mother's tomb. Outside the back door he paved the walk with two large mill-stones.'

30

St John's Well

BELOW Water and holy places are often allied, and such is the case here at Morwenstow. A level path crosses Morwenstow Churchyard from the porch of the Church to a private lane. Across the lane in an orchard stands St John's Well with its stone roof. Here is Max Tape, church treasurer, photographed by Ray Bishop on a May afternoon after several hours of energetic grass cutting. Max was born in Hawker's old cottage down in Coombe. 'As children, we called it "The Happy Valley",' Max recalls. This grand old well still provides clear spring water for baptisms at Morwenstow. It was already in use in the thirteenth century; though the well head is probably sixteenth century.

Rectory Farm

Hawker would surely have approved of Rectory Farm today standing on the southern side of the little green outside his Church. He would have approved of visitors and their donations in his box inside the Church – every coin is vital in preserving this lovely old building and in an age of tourism car parking space is very necessary. He would have approved too of the splendid homemade food on the Rectory Farm menu. Parts of Rectory Farm date back to the fourteenth century. In those days it was owned by the monks of the Hospital of St John at Bridgwater in Somerset. For clarification, Rectory is a

RIGHT An alcove in the dining room.

working farm, but the farmhouse makes visitors very welcome for food and drink from the spring through until autumn. The publisher of Bossiney Books makes regular visits to Morwenstow on book business and invariably takes refreshment in the character dining room. This was formerly the Rectory and history lives on in that nearby fields are known as church and glebe fields.

LEFT Part of the dining room at Rectory Farm – which is open to the public from spring until autumn. The photographs on the wall above the fireplace are members of the Waddon-Martyn family of Tonacombe Manor.

Parson Hawker

June Lander in her book *Eccentrics in Cornwall,* published by Bossiney back in 1983 and now out of print, included Hawker in her line-up of notable eccentrics.

From her chapter 'Parson Eccentrics' a vivid profile emerges:

'Whether Hawker actually acknowledged himself as an eccentric I do not know, but he certainly played up to visitors when his reputation became known. He told Sir Thomas Acland, a neighbour, that the bees on the cliffs picked up pebbles for ballast in high winds, dropping them at the entrance to their hives. He talked to the birds, giving them names like Jacky and Tommy; invited his nine cats into the Church, and is said to have excommunicated one of them for killing a mouse on Sunday; had a pig as a constant companion and kept a couple of deer, called Robin Hood and Maid Marion. A visiting Low Church clergyman calling at the Vicarage at Morwenstow was pinned to the ground by Robin's antlers, and had to be rescued by Hawker.

'But there was no doubt of his eccentricities in dress. Over a blue knitted fisherman's jersey, which had a small red cross woven into one side to mark the entrance of the centurion's spear, he wore a three-quarter-length claret or purple coloured coat. For extra warmth he would add a yellow poncho and scarlet gloves, or gauntlets. He had a variety of hats, including a black velvet cap, a pink, brimless fez-like hat, and a "wide-awake" of reddish brown.

'He wore large, black or brown sea boots up to his knees, and his socks, made out of the wool from his own ewe, were spun locally and knitted by girls at St Mark's School .... He carried a walking stick shaped like a sword, with a cross at the top, a flat, carpenter's pencil, a bunch of seals with religious symbols to press on the wax of his letters, and wore medallions, one of which had been blessed by a Cardinal.

'His indoor attire included a blue dressing gown, laced with gold braid, a vividly coloured biretta covered with sequins, and red slippers adorned with silver spangles.

'When one of his fellow clergymen commented on his dress, he replied: "At least I don't make myself look like a waiter or an unemployed undertaker."

'He had long hair – but hated beards; was proud of his ears which had no lobes – often remarking that the Duke of Wellington had ears of this shape, and that the feature could be traced in all the accurate pictures of Our Lord – and refused to wear false teeth when his own fell out, believing that all false teeth were taken by dentists from the jaws of human corpses, and that they "decayed sympathetically" with the bodies of their original hosts.

'His method of making tea was to fill the pot with tea leaves, and then pour the boiling water between the cracks. He liked the best ground coffee, but also loved cream – and was once discovered in the

dairy in the dead of night skimming off the cream from the previous day's milk with a spoon, and eating it as quickly as he could.

'He had thick, woven paper with faint red lines on it specially made for him by De La Rue, and wrote on it with swan quills; and when he was writing in his hut on the cliffs, which he had made out of wood from wrecked ships, he would take a basket of ready filled pipes with him, saying that tobacco was "the weed of thought".'

Hawker's Hut

ABOVE Hawker's Hut on the cliffs is probably the smallest property owned by the National Trust. Hawker built the original hut from driftwood which he hauled up from the beach below. This was his retreat. Here he wrote his poems and books, his songs and probably some of his sermons too. We know he often answered his mail here.

Hawker looked forward to his letters with the keen anticipation of a child at Christmas. When the postman passed by, without calling, he was bitterly disappointed. Each day was usually carefully mapped out, and on fine evenings he and his wife would wait for the postman who normally came around tea-time. They would then walk out to the hut, read his letters and answer them there on the spot. In his early days at Morwenstow he had to collect his letters from Shop, some two miles away, and he paid a girl two pence a week to fetch his mail.

Here too in his hut he sat and quietly smoked his pipes of opium and meditated. From this spot he also shaped his own weather forecasts, brooding on the possibilities of storm and shipwreck. This tiny building somehow personifies the man.

BELOW Dramatic aspect of the North Cornish cliffs at Morwenstow. In some curious way fine days are false to them. Ray Bishop, photographing them on a balmy spring afternoon, has captured that aloof quality which makes them so distinct – and menacing.

The Bush Inn

ABOVE Hawker, with his deep interest in Supernatural matters, would be intrigued to know The Bush Inn is one of the most haunted spots in the whole of the Westcountry. A dark shadowy figure moving away from the blazing building in 1968; footsteps, defying human explanation, both on the staircase and upstairs; ghostly knocking on a door which is no longer there; a Naval chaplain feeling 'menaced' in his four-poster bed at night; an American visitor encountering an elderly seafaring man, dressed in old-fashioned clothes, who, when challenged, simply turned and disappeared through a solid wall.

These are only some of the Supernatural happenings at The Bush. How the great man would have relished investigating such matters.

Interestingly nobody has suggested that Hawker himself haunts the inn, but we can be sure if he were alive today he would make a point of visiting The Bush at five in the morning or five in the evening – these being the haunted hours and BBC Radio Cornwall, visiting the inn in 1986, as part of its 'Ghost Hunt' series picked up sounds on tape, which defied all logical explanation.

BELOW The haunted stair case at The Bush Inn. Invisible footsteps – very distinct in sound – have been heard here many times over the years. Is it someone, from the past, leaving the building? Could they be part of some Supernatural tape recording from the past?

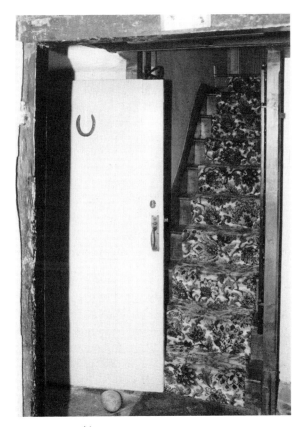

Hawker the Poet

Here are some examples of Hawker's handwriting made available for this publication by the Local Studies Library at Redruth. These pages concern his famous ballad *The Song of the Western Men* and an enlightening Note.

What are we to make of this handwriting?

It was Sir Walter Raleigh in the sixteenth century who reflected: 'That something of a man's character may be conjured from his handwriting ... the flourished capitals, do they not forcibly express the pride and sense of importance of the author?'

The strength and willpower of Robert Stephen Hawker shine from these pages: no hint of repression or reticence.

Would Hawker have become perhaps an even greater character, made a more substantial contribution to the Church and Life if he had lived elsewhere?

Such questions are inevitable. Sabine Baring-Gould possibly got to the heart of the matter when he wrote:

'Restricted to so narrow and isolated a sphere of action, his powers to some extent were perhaps wasted. With more scope he might have done greater things. As it was, his originality, independence of mind and eccentricities were contained and it is difficult to picture him living anywhere but at Morwenstow in that lonely valley by the cliffs within sound of the sea.'

Hawker, the poet. Where does he stand?

Baring-Gould rated him 'a poet of no mean order'. 'His ballads, and the poems inspired by the Cornish coast he loved, have the authentic ring of poetry,' was the verdict of Arthur Mee. 'With concentration, he might have been a notable poet, but he remains only a tantalising figure, aloof in his self-sufficiency and contradictions.' Ronald Duncan, a considerable wordsmith of these parts, confessed: 'To my taste Hawker's poems suffer from excessive use of both the vocative case and exclamation marks. But his prose has not these rhetorical defects ...'

Hawker's tour de force was *Quest of Sangreal.* Though overshadowed by Tennyson's *The Holy Grail,* it contains beautiful, powerful passages. In comparing the two, Baring-Gould said: '... if the two poems be regarded without previous knowledge of the name

The Song of the Western Men.

I

A good Sword and a trusty Hand!
   A merry Heart and true!
King James his men shall understand
   What Cornish Lads can do!

II

And have they fix'd the where and when?
   And shall Trelawny die?
Here's Twenty Thous-and Cornish men
   Will know the reason why!

III

Out spake their Captain brave and bold,—
   A merry Wight was he,—
If London Tower were Michael's Hold
   We'll set Trelawny free!
             And have &c

IV

We'll cross the Tamar, Land to Land!
   The Severn is no stay:
All side by side, and hand to hand,—
   And who shall bid us Nay?
             And have &c

V

And when we come to London Wall,
  A pleasant Sight to view, -
Come forth! Come forth! ye Cowards all!
Here's Men as good as you!

VI
                                    And have &c.
Trelawny He's in Keep and Hold,
  Trelawny He may die:
But here's Twenty Thousand Bold
  Will know the reason why!

R.S.H.

Note

With the exception of the refrain (Here's &c)
this Ballad was written by me, under Sir
Bevil's Oak, in Stowe Wood, in Nov.r 1824. It
was soon after inserted in a Plymouth Paper
without my Signature. It fell into the hands
of Mr Davies Gilbert, who sent a Copy to the
Gentleman's Magazine, under the impression,
that he had stumbled on the original Song.
It is also a matter of pride to me, that it
received the Praise of Sir W. Scott, as "a spirited
Ballad of the Seventeenth Century." Many
other Critics, and among them[+] The Percy
Society, and Charles Dickens, have recorded
their mistaken but complimentary persuasion
that it was the antique offspring of the Stuart age

+ Macaulay   R.S.H.

of their composers, I am not sure that some judges would not prefer the masterpiece of the Cornish poet . . .'

Though Tintagel was more than twenty miles away, Hawker was under the Arthurian spell. He had honeymooned there with Charlotte and made repeated visits: 'If I could but throw myself back to King Arthur's time.'

BELOW *The last photograph of Robert Stephen Hawker,* *taken before his departure to Plymouth – and his* *controversial death.*

King William's Bridge

RIGHT This is, in its way, a monument to the enterprise of Robert Stephen Hawker. The little river, that flows beneath it, is the natural boundary dividing the parishes of Morwenstow and Kilkhampton. Innocent as it may seem on most days, it can rise quickly in wet weather and in the early 1800s the ford was impassable in the worst flood conditions; but the plan to build a bridge foundered until the arrival of Hawker. Showing characteristic drive and determination, he opened a subscription list headed by no less than the King himself who donated twenty sovereigns to the cause. The bridge was built in 1836.

It was here that Hawker and Tennyson said farewell. Hawker accompanied Tennyson and Dr Dinham on their return journey to Bude as far as Coombe Valley. Tennyson left with these words: 'This is a day to be remembered ...' They never met again.

St Mark's School

LEFT St Mark's School at Shop is another kind of Hawker monument. By the year 1843, he had designed – in the form of a cross – and built the school. Outside all that, he furnished it at personal expense and provided a residence for the schoolmaster. The truth is the school was a constant drain on his finances, but he would be greatly heartened to find it still flourishing today. In this photograph, builders are at work on the extension in 1987.

RIGHT Even today this corner of North Cornwall has a somewhat 'secret' air, well personified by this leafy lane, frozen by the camera of Ray Bishop on a sunlit Sunday morning in June 1988.

Kilkhampton Church

LEFT Kilkhampton Church is on the busy A39. Kilkhampton and Morwenstow are adjoining parishes and Hawker took services here on a number of occasions – although he did not particularly like the parish. On one occasion he complained to the Bishop of Exeter that there were something like fifty Bible Christians inside the boundaries of Kilkhampton! Later he established good relations with the Reverend A. T. Thynne, the Rector of Kilkhampton who built a splendid vicarage, Penstowe Manor, in the 1860s. Hawker objected to the 'highly seasoned meat' served for dinner at Penstowe but nevertheless dined there frequently. The tower of Kilkhampton Church is a landmark for many miles. It stands some 500 feet above sea level. The great Purcell played the organ here, and it is interesting to reflect that on the black and white keys of Kilkhampton he almost certainly tried some of those famous anthems which have become such a part of British church music.

Stowe Barton

ABOVE Stowe Barton farm, a splendid farmhouse, built near the end of the eighteenth century from materials left from the demolition of Stowe, was once the proud home of the Grenvilles. Stowe itself has a curious and rather sad history. John Grenville, son of Sir Bevil, played a major role in restoring the Stuart monarchy, and was handsomely rewarded for his efforts. He became Earl of Bath, Governor of Plymouth, Lord Lieutenant of Cornwall and a Privy Councillor. Such rewards sharpened his social ambitions, and Stowe was rebuilt in 1679. A fine building, four storeys high, and boasting 365 windows, the great house stood for only a matter of six decades. A sequence of tragedy resulted in the last male heir departing this life in 1711. Sir Bevil's eldest daughter, for some reason or another, did not like Stowe, and ordered its demolition in 1739 – a ruthless method of avoiding the expense of running it.

RIGHT *Stowe Woods: beautiful but eerie.*

Penstowe

ABOVE Penstowe Manor, Kilkhampton, in 1988. Hawker often visited the Thynnes here. Initially critical of Mrs Thynne, Hawker however amended his view of the lady, later saying: '... should indeed feel desolate, but to have a friend near who is like an actual sister to my wife ...'

RIGHT A horse grazes peacefully in the grounds of Penstowe today. Carrow would have brought Hawker to Penstowe on various occasions. He later bought a grey pony for his second wife Pauline: 'an admirable match for Carrow', and they rode together a good deal, both in red boots. One suspects Hawker thought along John Wesley lines about animals and the Hereafter. Tackled by a Cornish farmer about an after-life for his favourite horse, Wesley replied: 'I hope there are horses in Heaven, but just in case they are not, then make his life here on Earth as good as possible.'

ABOVE The story goes that Coppinger emerged from a shipwreck and raging sea – ultimately brought ashore by a young woman horse rider, Dinah Hamlyn. They later married. Here is Paul Honeywill's drawing of the rescue.

Welcombe

BELOW St Nectan's Church at Welcombe. 'Welcombe. It is as if it were saying to the traveller coming from Cornwall, *Welcome into Devon,* for this lonely little place is at the Cornish border,' wrote Arthur Mee on a journey in the 1930s. The Church has a stumpy tower on the hill overlooking the glen which leads down to the cove. The screen inside the church is said to be the oldest in all Devon.

When Robert Stephen Hawker was made curate here, it must have been a lonely spot. Moreover he never forgot his encounter with the demon. Thereafter he sang hymns loudly whenever he rode through these valleys. The atmosphere of the place worked on his imagination too, for it is generally considered he based his novel *Cruel Coppinger* on this chunk of Westcountry coastline.

Cruel Coppinger, did he belong to fact or fiction?

Joy Wilson has contributed a perceptive chapter to *Westcountry Mysteries,* introduced by her husband Colin, and published by Bossiney.

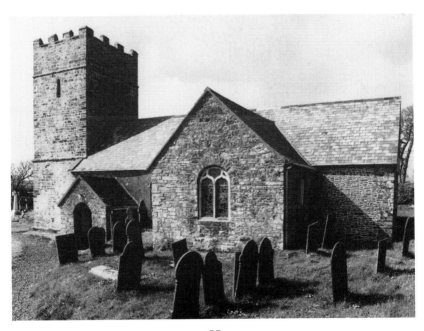

In it she writes: 'Was he just a satanic folk-hero? Is it safe to assume that "Cruel Coppinger" never existed? There are many documented facts which indicate that Coppinger really was in North Devon at that time. But the question is which Coppinger? Therein lies the mystery . . .

'In the year 1792 a certain Daniel Herbert Coppinger *is* recorded as landing from a shipwreck in Welcombe Parish. In Hartland Church entered in the register is his marriage with Dinah Hamlyn who was 42 at the time and not a young girl. There he is described as an officer of the King's Navy. But a check of the Navy List of the time does not show his name. An imposter perhaps?

'Scratched on the windowpane at Galsham, the house of his mother-in-law in Hartland parish, there is still to be seen a bold signature "D. H. Coppinger". His marriage does not seem to have been happy and in the course of time he is recorded in 1802 as a declared bankrupt, imprisoned in King's Bench prison for debt. He ended his life living at Barnstaple on a pittance from his estranged wife. Mrs Coppinger lived to 1833 and lies buried beside her mother in Hartland Church.

'But can the man with this rather ineffectual lifestory be the model for Cruel Coppinger?

'Perhaps not . . .'

LEFT *The Welcombe font, drawn by Felicity Young. In the eye of our imagination we can somehow see the Reverend Hawker performing the service of baptism here. St Nectan, Patron of the parish, was a Welsh hermit who came to Hartland in the sixth century.*

RIGHT *The Devil's Door and the well at Welcombe.*

ABOVE This screen at Welcombe is reputed to be the oldest in the county of Devon. It is certainly an impressive piece of Devonshire craftmanship. Welcombe Church began life as a chapel attached to Hartland Abbey. It was not until the year 1508 that Welcombe became 'an independent parish'. Inside the Church today you can see a deed, dated 1532, in which the local parishioners agreed to provide a priest, and the Abbey paid the princely sum of £5 yearly: a contribution to his income.

Coombe

RIGHT Coombe, photographed by Ray Bishop on a beautiful May afternoon in 1988. This lovely hamlet, in many ways scarcely changed in atmosphere since Hawker's day, is maintained by the Landmark Trust. Several of these Coombe cottages are available for summer lets – ideal places for recharging of batteries in our hectic last quarter of the twentieth century. The tiny river here makes the natural boundary between Kilkhampton and Morwenstow.

LEFT Hawker's cottage at Coombe. He must have been happy in this lovely secluded valley. Hawker and his wife lived here when he was studying for Holy Orders. An interesting legacy is the window he built in the shape of a cross. It consists of small panes of glass to let maximum light into his study. Hawker claimed the holy light encouraged and inspired him and, for all his life, the cross was a mystical symbol.

Duckpool

ABOVE Duckpool even today has the air of the place that smugglers might have used. In this neck of the Westcountry Woods, the only major river valley is that which emerges at Duckpool. How did Duckpool get its name? Well, the theory is they ducked witches here!

Two aspects of the coastline at Morwenstow and Welcombe Mouth. Truly these cliffs are too savage to be called pretty, too cruel to earn an adjective like beautiful. Ronald Duncan, who as a writer was born with a silver spoon in his mouth, once reflected it was a great relief to stand on these northern cliffs. In his opinion they seemed 'to despise and defy humanity'.

Also Available

NORTH CORNWALL IN THE OLD DAYS
Joan Rendell

SUPERNATURAL ADVENTURE
Michael Williams

COASTLINE OF CORNWALL
Ken Duxbury

THE CRUEL CORNISH SEA
David Mudd

GHOSTS OF CORNWALL
Peter Underwood

LEGENDS OF CORNWALL
Sally Jones

SEA STORIES OF CORNWALL
Ken Duxbury

E.V. THOMPSON'S WESTCOUNTRY

HIDDEN KNOWLEDGE
Lori Reid

HISTORIC INNS OF CORNWALL
Colin Gregory

WESTCOUNTRY MYSTERIES
Introduced by Colin Wilson

SUPERNATURAL IN CORNWALL
Michael Williams

We shall be pleased to send you our catalogue giving full details of our growing list of titles for Devon, Cornwall, Dorset and Somerset as well as forthcoming publications. If you have difficulty in obtaining our titles, write direct to Bossiney Books, Land's End, St Teath, Bodmin, Cornwall.